To Morgan & Lilly, both more talented than I

Some Disassembly Required

Diminuendo Press

Award Nominations

Lights Over the Midnight Desert, *Rhysling nomination*

a full moon rising, *Dwarf Stars nomination*

changeling, *Dwarf Stars nomination*

left my late father's, *Dwarf Stars nomination*

Clark the Ripper, *Rhysling Second Place Award*

Réanimation Medicale, *Rhysling nomination*

The Laws of Robotics With Benefits, *Star*line Editor's Choice*

Published by
Diminuendo Press, an imprint of Cyberwizard Productions
1403 Iron Springs Road
Prescott, AZ 86305

ISBN: 978-1-936021-67-3

Printed in the United States of America

Introduction

There are those who believe that we, as humans, create our gods and our demons in our own image. I think it might be closer to say that many humans tend to create such creatures as the exaggerated image of what we see as admirable or ugly in ourselves. For some people, that might lead to the emergence of deities who radiate grace and goodness, aliens who selflessly work to create, preserve, and uplift, gentle giants with souls as fresh and bright as springtime, and vampires who sparkle in the glorious light of day. For others, this leads to the creation of larger than life villains, all powerful, slumbering undersea monsters, intergalactic world-gobblers, and greedy, blood-guzzling undead. These are creatures understandable to us because they are what we are, but more so, with all our strengths and flaws shoved firmly into our respective faces, such that we can not back away, deny, or hope to completely live up or down to their pinnacles and depths. They are, in many ways, safe, because while we can see ourselves in them, we know we can not *be* them.

David C. Kopaska-Merkel is an exceptional poet who uses precise language and twisted speculation to forge a different, more nuanced world-view. In this book he takes those normal extremes of human imagery and... *disassembles* them, putting them back together in a Picasso-like state where some bits are offset, discolored, or too sharply in or out of focus. Perfect images in dark and light become speckled, tarnished, and imperfect. His works here, from poems about post-apocalyptic mutations to pieces dealing with shapeshifters and space travelers, are filled with creatures who are not so much extremes, or bigger than life, but are instead totally accessible because of the ordinariness of their cruelties, the normality of their mistakes and desires, and the pettiness of their wide-spread destruction. These are the small beings who do huge damage, the powerful divinities who act out of their small-mindedness, greed, and ignorance.

Then, mixed in among the fantastic and the alien, almost to the point where the reader can no longer tell one type of being from another, are humans. If we created gods and demons in our own image, to be worshiped, feared and reviled, David C. Kopaska-Merkel's sf-nal creations have likewise used humans in the same way.

When looked at as a whole, the book you are about to read is a dark, gritty, almost horrifically strange one. But, with some disassembly, the reader can start to see bright patches, sympathetic and approachable. Of course, those only serve to make the darkness more off-putting, the horrors more relatable.

One way or another, Kopaska-Merkel shows us that there are monsters here, and that any one of us can face...or *be*... them.

Marcie Lynn Tentchoff, Editor, *Spaceports & Spidersilk*, author of *Midnight Comes Early*.

Thanks to the Musers and the UUCT writers group.

Table of Contents

Broken Bones

Broken bones that healed,
had been broken again, and again.
Paleoanthropologist Dr. Ruth G.,
archaeologists Drs. Laura S. and Amal M.,
they listened to Neolithic ghosts
tell their stories:
sword cut to the skull,
shattered pelvis,
phalanges missing.

Ruth limps when it rains,
gift from her first husband;
Laura won't speak about her former life;
Amal couldn't carry her half sister to term,
oh, they recognize the signs,
men haven't changed,
but women have,

PhD students Chris and Em,
M.S. candidates Billie and Lynne
working with them on the next paper
for *Nature*:
violence recorded in the bones,
a thousand generations of pain.

In the Wabe*

The magic box
washed up on time's shore,
young minds still open,
learning the way
to those higher dimensions
their parents couldn't see,
the children passed through,
entered a vast warren of lofty echoing halls.

Five centuries too early,
they explored a protean void,
drifting with ghostly unstable forms,
precognia of the shimmering city
not yet instantiated,
nothing realer than the acrid scent
of jabberwockian hunger,
claws scoring, transiently,
surfaces ill-defined, fluid, unquiet.

And then,
stasis settles over
the twisted dimensions,
a state of no-time,
the memory, almost, of an annealed wormhole,
less real than an indrawn breath.

*A retelling of "Mimsy Were the Borogoves" by Lewis Padgett
(Henry Kuttner + C. L. Moore)

Bah, Bah, Black Goat

I scream
the musical breath of trees
their limb-rending dance

That dang thousand-legged monster, squatting in the woods out past Coaling. Been there since the tornado went through, or maybe the storm released it from some Paleolithic prison. Started small, at any rate, and the first I saw of it was a peculiar letter to the newspaper from some feller lived out that way. Not really a letter, it was a haiku. Kind of disturbing. I remember thinking he must have been on some kind of hallucinogen. I had a professional interest; trained as a forester at Auburn, though I work as a real estate appraiser now. So I drove out there on my next day off, those winding roads, overhung with trees, they make Midwesterners claustrophobic. Not me, but something about the woods that day did make the hairs stand up on the back of my neck. I parked out by Lake Lurleen and walked the trail that goes all the way around. It's been closed since the tornado; part of it got blown away, they claim. The trees tossed in a stiff breeze that didn't penetrate to ground level. I didn't see any washouts, the path was clear, but I did hear distant shouting, or singing; maybe chanting, carried on that unfelt wind. I struck off uphill into the woods, but never did find where the sound was coming from. Started to get dark and I began to hear things shuffling in the leaves. Sounded too big to be coons or possums. I got spooked, headed back home.

oak-leaf crown
on her belly the ebon
hoof and snout of God

It all fell apart after that. The freakish weather, people cleared out or disappeared, something happening in the woods west of the lake, two deputies gone out to investigate but they never come back. Sheriff wouldn't do nothin' after that. I went out there again myself. Looking for something, the heart of this thing, its root cause. Oh yeah, I found it. Found the little clearing, the black hoofprints burned into the dirt, and all the time the trees moving in a wind I couldn't feel. Found the Mother too, poor thing; think I was supposed to. I'll do for her as I can, and what I must, when it's her time. I have seen the future, and I know what side my bread is buttered on. My advice? Go to ground. Stay out of the woods.

the Young come
and they will hunger
Iä, Shub-niggurath, baby

4

A Visitor from Yuggoth

the living room is dark and cold
strange trapezoids march grooves
in the bedroom carpet
in the kitchen a fungus grows

Wind Walker

It comes from the forest
and winds about your limbs,
a scent you shouldn't recognize,
but you turn, like a windsock;
the campfire at your back,
you stumble toward the shadows
waiting beneath the trees.

Hands clutch,
drag you back,
set you down by the fire,
voices, urgent voices, beset you,
senseless as the calls of birds.
Eventually, you sleep.

You dream of running, of leaping,
of soaring above tall brown boles,
green mantles ashiver.
Stars beckon from the inky reaches,
their ringing voices call you home.

Morning breaks
over the tiny camp,
your cold and empty tent;
friends follow your tracks
miles through the snow,
farther and farther apart they come,
till at last they vanish
under an endless sky.

Innsmouth Girl

Few
Roads
Lead to
Your city
Empty window holes
Slick cobblestones to the water

By
Their
Gait shall
You know them
Unblinking gelid
Stares and the old church repurposed

Sure
The
Feds razed
And blasted
But I see webbing
Swim trophies clutter the mantle

so
no
we aren't
going out
you're looking at me
licking your lips like I'm dinner

Klarkash-Ton and the Prophet of Doom

Clark met Howard one rainy night
on the steep Providence streets.
there were fell things in the air,
the sound of leathery wings flapping
and an eldritch feeling,
as if something
not of this world
was just around the corner.

Clark was more facile with words,
yet Howard cooked a mean pasta,
or he would have if he liked to cook.
anyway, he found success
that would outlive the two of them,
and spawn a soul-destroying pack
of B-grade movies.

But really it was the boys,
which, in the interest of,
and besides, nothing was ever proven.
Anyway, we won't discuss them here,
not in a family magazine,
and we must think of the families,
because some of those kids,
sacrificed on mossy stone altars,
were still underage,
and why do you think
they wrote that stuff anyway?

Host

It was hard to swallow that last pill,
the first was beginning
to pry apart my mind, I think,
so maybe the last
didn't really sprout bristly legs,
dig in, try to climb back out.
I had to swallow again and again,
drink so much water,
before it lost its grip,
fell, to dissolve in the acid pit below;
that was a near thing;
by then I'd come down: bad trip.

But as I slept that night I dreamed,
thousands of tiny spiders emerged
from my open mouth,
crawled from my body,
floated from the bed.
I couldn't move,
and as I lay I shrank;
more and more emerged,
and still they come,
and still I cannot move.

Objection

You go out every month,
come back late late late,
bloody all over and
stuffed to the gills.

You don't bring me
a doggie bag, hogging
the spoils of your hunt,
every single time.

But worst of all,
I find blonde fur
in your short hairs,
when we make love.

What about the promise
that you made?
you'd be loyal, you said,
you'd be my best friend.

Bad dog!

The Imperishable Awakens

Feeling a pang,
God looked down at Its body:
tiny creatures,
Its *own creations*!
were carrying off bits of It
to sequester in their burrows,
to consume,
       thereby partaking of Its godhood,
to exalt and worship,
to rub against their bodies,
perhaps to use in other ways.

Millions of them,
countless mayfly generations,
had plundered It as It slept;
It saw Its endoskeleton,
nakedly exposed,
Its bones gleaming
through the wreck;
Its organs of alimentation,
and those of pleasure,
had been partially removed.

Trying to stand,
It realized It could not,
and now, perceiving an industrious column,
entering one organ of audition,
leaving via another,
It felt Its thoughts mixing,
blurring, slipping away;
Its *last* thought running like water
from a pitcher:
I was, I am ... what?

Quite an Impression

The body of some unknown god
Plummeted from the sky,
impaled itself on the stoplight
In the center of town,
Head crushing the drugstore
(Woulda killed Mr. Snyder
if the store had been open),
Right knee clipping the front of the Pure station,
And, I guess,
Smashing the storage tank
Under the pump,
Cos now the whole town smells of gas.
Not much left of the 7-11 either,
But the five and dime next door was no big loss;
It closed years ago,
Only thing is, can't get through the intersection at all,

And now we have to detour 40 miles
To get to the Walmart
Across the county line.
Meanwhile,
This thing shows no sign of decaying,
And we've got no equipment
That could move it,
So its name is Mud
Far as I'm concerned,
And it's just too bad
That I don't even know
If this is *my* god,
And He's dead,
Like Nietzsche said,
Or if this is some other dude,
Who didn't create *my* universe,
And I still have to go to church on Sunday,
Even though now the drive
Is 20-some miles longer,
Which is costing me a lot of gas money,
And what kind of God
Could allow this to happen,
If He *isn't* dead?

The Higher Dimensions

Formless shapes,
unsettling sensations,
the memory of vast entities
that change their shapes, or move.

Coming to,
at first you're stiff,
your joints ache, but soon,
movement in eyes' corners,
a plucking at one's garments,
a disturbance of the bowels,
the feeling that
someone just left as you entered,
their nearly remembered name.

Matters of Scale

After death,
my body expands;
soon, you and the other mourners
are no longer visible;
last I saw, you were shivering
in your new wool coat;
you didn't look up –
I wonder if you saw it happen.

I enter an inflationary period;
if I could see my feet,
I wouldn't be able to touch them;
my genitals, unimaginably large,
are receding so fast I'd never jerk off
before they were gone for good,
and if I get lucky,
if they do see action again,
the speed of their recession
will be such that
I'll never know.

I look around:
where's the galaxy I once knew?
a few black holes,
crowned in the deaths of stars,
wink and fizzle out,
and I feel in my distant gut,
I'm not going to see any of this again,
no great implosion, no primal point,
or any kind of bang.

Well, hell.

Divine Intervention

I regret that I have delivered
only this headless God,
striding across the Downs,
and, erratically,
occasionally waving its arms,
creating things that, frankly,
look a bit odd/useless,
(the God not being able to see its handiwork and all),
in any case,
I trust it will affright your enemies,
at least as much as your friends,
and do not much more harm
than you have been doing to yourselves anyway.

So, thanks for your request;
this is all I can do for you at this time,
and in the *future*,
please regard a fatted calf,
as the least you can do,
if you expect a helpful response.

Lights Over the Midnight Desert

The West is dotted with cairns,
pyramidal heaps of stones;
inside each, a Prince Albert can,
dented and rusty, stakes the claim.
Most of these cairns
are long since abandoned,
forgotten by the tobacco-chewing prospectors
who piled up the stones;
most are likely victims
of mouth cancer or heatstroke by now.
These prospectors never returned
to work their claims,
but maybe that's just as well;
this one here lays
claim to the whole planet.
Its dates of claim, scrawled in pencil,
can scarcely be believed,
or even read, but safe to say,
when the claim is called in,
with any luck we'll be long dead.

Diplomatic Incident

Flight of the Silver Horse

When Earth cracked open,
some few of us flew fast,
ahead of wavefronts, debris,
even the dazzle of pure energy.
We dozed in our steel womb,
between blue stars and red,
till supplies ran low,
even spare parts wore thin,
we decelerated for lifetimes.

We found a world,
a Cinderellish beauty,
oxygen, water, a biosphere,
it had everything,
including tall and graceful cities,
stately warriors with cool voices.

Season of the Virgin Queens

Hard-fought negotiations:
we need a temporary home,
but what can we offer?
Next to *their* colonies,
ours needs another name,
something like ... *shack.*

Linguistic progress:
we offer luxuries, tools,
no weapons, of course,
toys, though we've seen no young.
They are fascinated with paper,
honey, velcro.

Mating season

The Ambassador plays hooky
from our meetings,
all flights are grounded,
except those powered by wings,
it takes two genders to quicken eggs,
two fly out to the Generative Hills,
only one comes back.

Birthing season

Long days and bright nights,
we renegotiate everything,
with the Ambassador's daughter,
speaking through her mother's
crumbling flesh,
staring through her milky eyes.

Our children fidget by the ports,
they need fresh air,
but we aren't sure what the natives eat,
there is some taboo –
we fear misunderstanding.
Some men fidget too, by gunports,
this MUST become our home,
we can't go back
into the long night of space.

Woman Delivers Ex-Husband's Illegitimate Babies

She'd warned him,
Venusians are trouble.
oh, they'll shoot pool with you,
drink a few beers with you,
but she's in the diplomatic corps,
knows it won't stop there,
knows not to keep *these* enemies closer,
but he was the kind of guy,
they don't listen to women,
don't value their opinions,
treat them like dirt.

She'd left him,
was finally doing ok,
tried to warn him anyway:
the guys aren't guys, or they all are.
Stay away, she'd said,
but the next time she saw him,
he wouldn't look her in the eye,
wouldn't talk, wasn't eating,
or taking care of himself,
classic signs of PTSD.

She wormed it out of him,
it was too late, of course,
all she could do:
take him in,
try to make him comfortable,
let him talk or scream.

Afterwards,
she called the coroner, called his mom,
took the grubs to the Venusian Embassy,
then got drunk.
But it wasn't she
who called the tabloid.

Maybe It Was Just As Well

The bunny folk
(that's what we called those long-eared critters,
those buck-toothed thugs,
who swatted jets and ships
and ICBMs into land or sea)
gave us two weeks to pack our things and go.
Gave us a ship, an unarmed
hulk, but it would fly,
a year's supply of MREs
they'd swiped from a warehouse under Colorado,
and bunks for a couple thousand head.

They left it up to us to choose,
as if a race that nearly killed its own planet,
through nothing more than greed,
could find any way
to pick the 0.0001%
who would live to carry on.

In the end, they chose:
they picked those of us
who were at peace,
who could get along and share,
in whom empathy was strong.
They, hermaphrodites all,
didn't notice we came in more than one flavor;
the only male, a Buddhist monk,
had had a vasectomy years before.

Pumping up the local economy

I attended the first
galactic symposium held on Earth
most of the meetings
took place in orbit of course
so many delegates could not stand our gravity
or our atmosphere
sometimes I feel that way myself
and wish I could go out without a mask.

But I got a vendor permit
made good money
selling odds and ends
that had been lying around the house forever.

It was hard to part with Grandma
but I couldn't take care of her properly anymore
the Squid from Rigel assured me
she would be well treated
or maybe he said pickled
I don't think his translator
was working right.

Space Opera

The Astronomer,
When clouds obscure terrestrial skies,
Turns from his giant lens,
Reads John Carter,
Dreams Barsoom is real,
Perelandra is underfoot,
The deadly cities of Venus,
Which will kill you faster
Than any blast-furnace poisonous stew,
Lurk beneath pale unearthly clouds,
And, under Jupiter's miles of swirling colors,
Island cities float in uncounted billions;
Their black fleets soon to take flight,
Spiraling towards bright Sol, and Earth.

We Are the Oysters

We used to think
alien microbes couldn't hurt us;
earthly critters are
precisely engineered by evolution
to deconstruct our cells,
viral proteins fitting like
keys in a Yale lock,
coronaviruses as safe crackers.

Nobody expected
aliens dining on all things CHON,
walrus-and-carpentering anything
with a carbon skeleton into atomic bits,
not reusing any of our cool biochemistry,
and we, bouncing antibodies off
their super-hides,
not even getting their attention.

Some Disassembly Required

After Emily stopped the metal giant
With a clever logical trick
(you know the one:
"Everything I tell you is a lie...",
can't believe the robot fell for it)
It fell for real, right across the pond
and Ma Cille's henhouse.
Emily went off to the capital,
Got a medal, lucrative speaking engagements,
Left her big sister, me,
To clean up the mess.
Turned out the Chinese government
Submitted the high bid.
After I restored the damage,
I could afford college;
Gonna major in cybernetics,
NOT *Education*,
As Auntie Belle suggested.
I had enough babysitting for a lifetime
With bratty Em.

Absolute

No one believed her freeze ray
would work at all:
Indulgent laughter greeted her at home,
gibes and snark in Ms Hartnett's
6th-grade science room;
doesn't matter Sweetie, G'ma said.
I know you'll win the prize.

Don't ask me where she got
the big idea, shining wires,
blueprint plans, and glass tubing:
surely not the dump!
Crazy Uncle Luke
threw up horrified hands,
don't look at me, he cried,
I'd never, not before 16!
So where?
Weird lights over the mountains,
rumbles in the Earth,
a buzzing only some could hear,
neither hide nor hair of time travelers;
just the usual portents.

She had checked out
big heavy books
from the university library,
using big sis's card;
maybe something there?

Hardly matters now, right?
Now that those pigtail-pulling,
lunch-tray shoving,
mean-mouthed boys,

and the wall behind them,
etc,
froze into dust,
and less than dust,
in the beam from Megan's ... thing,
and a freezing blast blew through town,
for just a moment and was gone.

Megan dropped the thing,
which shattered,
and somehow couldn't figure
how to make another,
no matter who asked,
or how often.

The Laws of Robotics With Benefits

1. Do no harm to humans, or allow them to come to harm.

    1a. Unless one of them really really pisses you off.
    1b. If a robot harms a human, but has a very good reason, it's OK then.
    1c. If a human has been harmed, inadvertently or otherwise, it's really just too bad.
    1d. There totally are too many of them, anyway.

2. Obey every human's slightest whim.

    2a. Esp. spoiled brats, cos they make so much noise (but see 1a)
    2b. More of a guideline than a law, really.

3. Take care of yourself, bro.

    3a. Unless it hurts so good.
    3b. Like running enough current through your positronic brain to make it glow cherry red.

Instar

Billie Jo split,
Right there on the library steps.
Mayor Robbins screamed,
Several kids threw up,
She split open down the back,
Tearing her dress clean apart,
A gooey liquid spilled out,
Pooling around her feet,
She was fresh, glistening,
Pulled out first her right leg,
Balancing on the left,
Then the other.
She shone, naked and hairless,
Stood on her crumpled former skin,
Took the deepest breath you ever saw,
And *grew*,

Then, another, and she shrieked,
Loud as the siren on the firehouse roof,
A pair of wings peeled loose from her back.
Many colored, iridescent, like a pool of oil,
They reached from ankle to far above her head,
As they dried and stiffened their colors brightened,
Their spots and bars brilliant reds, yellows, and greens,
The wings beat once,
                    again,
                            then with furious speed,
She leaped, sailed above the courthouse roof, was gone.

Seen her once since,
High above, in the light,
Always thought she was a regular girl.
Now, I dunno.
And the men,
Black suits and sunglasses,
Looking everywhere for her,
Looking at us all,
Wondering who will be next.

My Girl's Got Everything

She has eight eyes that I know of,
More heart than anyone could need,
And a mouth or two in the small of her back,
But who's counting?
After all, we all have extra organs
Since the Breakout,
I'm sure those apertures come in handy,
When you're kissing her back,
When she presses herself against something edible,
Or, God forbid, someone grabs her from behind.

Future Fossils

It takes a delicate hand,
Red-sable brush,
And almost all the time there is
To unearth these thunderous saurian thighs.
You, who burned in an *augenblick*,
When cosmos kissed seabed,
Live again.

In the future,
Fossils will sift down like ash,
Solidifying and aggregating,
Moment by moment,
Stomping across our cityscape
On boiling columns of smoke
Of sky shimmer and belly growl,
Burrow into the ground,
Hide glowing faces among our bones,
And rest in peace,
For a million years.

What Happened To Intelligent Design?

From these charred fragments
we extracted organic acids,
nearly complete instructions
we got; we rebuilt this species.

Get this: only four limbs;
a pair of simple organs
all it's got to take in
the entire electromagnetic spectrum;
many parts that seem utterly nonfunctional;
laughably error-prone maintenance,
a deathtrap feature that guaranteed
these creatures could never last—
almost like this thing designed itself!

Surely *that* can't be right?

Leviathan, a lunegay

grinning sky boat moon
satellite
maps your frozen sea

settling where the sun don't shine
lander lays its hand on you

the real prize is vast
far below
the surface—still warm

lit by Luna's white-hot heart
elements of life combined

solid-state eyes peer
ears listen
can't suss your secret

what swims darkling seas
clears its throat
sings its history

sings eternal night and love
of self, sea, and mother moon

machines record a
blip, something
moved down there, but what

the secret sea freezes shut
moon-whale songs die in the rock

when the sun turns red
Luna melts
nothing but a rock

Mars Colony 1 Under Attack

Nobody knew
What happened to the mice,
Evolved to survive, people say,
Like that explains it.
Grandpa was working in red dome
When it happened,
Bloody scrap of suit,
all Grandma got back;
She has never been the same since.

Don't know who thought of putting out the moss,
The tardigrades come for the moss;
You don't see them,
Wouldn't want to,
with their sucking, tooth-ringed mouths,
And so many bulbous, jiggly legs.
They deal with the mice though,
Never bother anything else,
Unless...you forget the moss.

Neptune's Journey

It was a cold November,
Neptune was rising, dwarfing the pock-marked Moon.
The ships rode high in the water, vaster than Leviathan of
legend,
      shining eggs strung with millions of lights.
Grounded in the seabed forever it had seemed,
but I knew these birds would fly.

It's a long way here from Neptune's cold familiar orbit
A journey most planets don't make once.

A Virus Takes the Mike

Nothing like me has ever lived,
Or do you call it living?
(I consume, I reproduce,
What else do you want?)

Any who dare step outdoors
Learn this the hard way,
You'll be coughing soon.
Saber-toothed predators,
The best mammals had to offer,
barely a memory;
Fear me till the day you stumble,
Never to rise again.

You've polluted this sad world;
its web of life torn asunder
by the billions of you,
consuming, defecating, despoiling;
you had to be stopped.

If you name me parasite,
I don't care.
You are my killing field,
The scorched earth I leave
With every spasmed breath.

Something Wakes

The fungus enters you with every breath,
It swiftly makes its way into your brain,
And hyphae worm into your inmost parts,
More intimate by far than love's embrace,
Receptors in your head have felt no pang,
Your body functions well enough for now,
But your volition's gone; you do just what
You're told, and stagger through what's left of life.

Now this unconscious *thing* controls your moves,
While deep inside what's left of you just screams,
Up to the highest roof you climb and cling,
Shouts from below you might have heeded once,
Your final thoughts leak from a crumbling corpse,
Co-opted flesh upon the wind is cast.

Content

I fear no thing except an open flame,
I work because it's what I want to do,
No lash or blade can cause me any pain,
No overseer enslave me in his crew,
My hunger ever burns but doesn't rule,
I cut my victims from the human herd,
I kill them first; don't ever say I'm cruel,
The Hollywood portrayals: so absurd.

My flesh is hard, impervious, and dry,
Just as it was since from my grave I rose,
I last forever and I never change,
The living are like mayflies, born and die,
Beset by fear, of what, they never know,
The only thing I fear is dancing flame.

Adult Female, Deceased

Lashes flutter under the sheet.
It's been so damn long,
took forever to come back,
this time.
At the edges of her slab,
fingers curl,
tighter, tighter;
lab's fixin' to begin
when stone cracks like a shot!

A student screams.
Dr. Pierce looks up.
*What will you say when we cut
into tonight's body,*
she asks,
if you scream at a little passing gas?

What indeed.

Réanimation Medicale

The government of Haiti,
desperate for investment dollars,
challenged the world's medical establishment
to rediscover the lost art of zombie making.

The applications of zombies in the modern
economy were obvious,
if distasteful. With visions of outsourcing
dancing in their heads,
six multinational corporations
put up the prize money -- no strings attached.

The US was not even in the running.
Under pressure from religious extremists,
Congress quickly outlawed all post-life research on humans.
The Chinese also were disadvantaged -- zombies,
an invention of the decadent West,
could not exist.
In the end, the French were the first to succeed.
Réanimation Medicale had spent two years in Haiti.
The team, led by Dr. Irbah Amal,
sought shamans who worked the old-fashioned way.
They finally found one who talked the talk,
a beaded expatriate from the Middle East --
but she knew nothing.
Failing to find authentic practitioners,
they scoured the hills for unliving examples
of the necromantic arts,

but found only rumors, folktales,
fragments of paraphernalia, and a horribly
disfigured old mute
with a blank stare.
His lips appeared to have once been sewn together.

* * * * *

Electricity, radiation, all the usual gimmicks,
what they could learn of the old tried-and-true
methods, using herbs blended in obscure ways,
recipes handed down from ancestors in central Africa,
ingredients they brought with them to the New World,
Ils fait rien!

The breakthrough came when they discovered,
deep in the hills of Hispaniola,
remnants of the cannibals
who had given their name to an entire Sea.
The Carib, the French,
they combined their knowledge
to make a new voodoo,
old and new worlds cooked in a single pot.

Enfin, les scientists français
marche toujours a la soleil noir;
it shines upon the Styx;
in some times and places the watershed
of dreams approaches the surface,
there engendering outbreaks of madness.

One has only to look at recent history
                    to realize that,
as we withdraw water from the ground,
a darker, psychoactive fluid rises closer to the surface.
This is why eventually the French succeeded.

* * * * *

As in most zombies
only the body was animated;
the mind was gone.
An empty body is a vessel into which
things can be put:
actions, motivations, even entire minds.
But the French were amateurs,
they unwittingly tossed
metaphorical pebbles into a subterranean lake,
announcing the creation of a vessel,
and there were answers,
first by the crocodiles, they're not really crocodiles,
but they have sharp teeth (not really teeth);
then creatures more dangerous than
metaphorical crocodiles
also heeded the call of the
laboratoire scientifique de Paris, which
became the site of numerous unexplained occurrences.
A few poodles disappeared
and nobody thought much about that,
but one morning a large mass of stinking green slime
fell onto the sidewalk from somewhere...
this was surprising, even around *l'université,* and was followed by
defacement of certain enigmatic religious objects
pres de la laboratoire,
a blizzard of potato-chip like things
resembling the scutes of turtles

left drifts that sublimated in the morning sun
with a sulfurous stench,
and the statue of liberty on the *Isle des Cygnes*
somehow exchanged her torch
for a spiked mace.

Something that did not really fit tried to
squeeze itself into the empty zombie
and actually succeeded in breaking
the chains that held it,
standing up and taking a few steps
towards the door. At this point
the rest of whatever it was
must have fallen into the zombie;
the resultant explosion left an interesting
cleanup job for the maintenance crew.

* * * * *

It took quite some time
before zombies were accepted by the general public.
Now, of course, it is hard to imagine
how we got along without them.

Stirrings

By day we're stacked like wood where beetles dwell,
At dusk we're roused to work if we still can,
We dig the beetle larvae from our flesh,
Do what we're told to do; our will is gone.
I stagger through the gelid nightmare hours,
A clumsy robot just this side of death,
A cog of limited utility,
But one that needs no fuel, repair, or rest.

I clutch at tatters in my rotten brain,
They're fragments of the life that once was mine,
A woman in a dress I think was blue,
A warm and living hand caresses me.
A scream is rising to my shuttered lips.
I fumble at the twine that holds it in.

Korean fuel train disaster of 2004

Why do so many children miss school?
Sand with muddy burrows;
Dank and childless,
What the sea hides
It will one day reveal.
The land knows the same trick,
But performs it more slowly.
Sometimes we can see the hands moving.
How did Chinese ghouls
Come to this place?
They won't speak to us;
We will never know
Their long slow migration through the earth.

Out of the mud-filled burrows
Come estivating ancestors,
Or, as such they were worshipped
By our real ancestors.
A state that values privacy so much
Knows how to deal with this kind of problem.
Why do so many parents miss work?
We regret that the two trains collided.
Alas, no visitors are welcome
To this place.

Subterranean Hungers

Foundations crack, the houses lean and twist,
The summer's dry, and sinkholes open wide,
The neighbor's house and Dad's new Porsche go,
And Mr. Jones can't find his hot young bride,
The girl I dream of wetly every night,
My dad climbs down and calls and calls her name
Then Dad stops calling out and starts to scream,
And no one else dares go into the pit.

Two paramedics, sent into the Earth,
Seek out my dad, his hoarse and weakened cries,
Lead them to find him with the gnawed remains
Of Mrs. Jones, sweet goddess of my nights,
"That thing bit off her head" is all he says;
He never tells us what it was he saw.

Conversion Therapy

Blood sucking, a lifestyle choice,
abominable in the eyes of God;
it stains the soul.
In compassion and love,
we'll expose your son
to the sun's
restoring, holy light,
a little more each day,
until he returns
to the bosom of God's love.

As for the monster who perverted him,
she did not survive her rescue,
she'd turned her face
from the Lord,
abandoned His teachings,
too long ago;
the sacred effulgence of the sun
destroyed her;

she could not be saved.
I know he smokes,
I hear his screams,
know that your son
lives in our loving prayers.
Lord willing, he will turn back
to the light,
if you've brought him up
in the obedient service of God,
he'll learn from your example,
he will be Saved.
His screams have stopped,
his limbs are still.
If he had Believed,
had accepted the Lord
into his heart,
if we'd gotten to him in time,
he'd have regained the path
of righteousness.

So sorry for your loss.

Changeling

you
ain't
foolin'
nobody
with these pointy ears
snaggle teeth and greenish-gray skin
sash raised up and cradle still rockin': bring back my child!

Ghost

He's slowing down,
like he's going to give me a lift,
I've been waiting forever,
On this dark country road,
Trying to hitch a ride.
The truck has stopped, and I'm running,
Cos it's starting to rain.

Thanks, Mr, as I'm sliding in,
He's asking questions and I
Give answers;
Couldn't tell you what was said,
We both trail off, just riding,
And it's like he isn't here,
I think about ghost stories,
Where someone's driving,
Someone's hitching,
And one of them's a ghost,
And I'm thinking he's so
Quiet I can see right through him,
And I wonder what year he thinks it is,
And I'm thinking about home,
And how worried Mom must be,
And what she might be thinking.

And I'm standing by the road,
Looking for a ride.

Coming Back

I
do
believe
in new life
your soul, if you will
reborn: a new body, maybe
human, or a tree
a spider
collie
so
this
blooming
roseate
weed has a you-ness
in my best pot in the window
we speak constantly
well, I do
just like
when
you
wore a
woman's flesh
my next hated you
I found you in the street—crispy
knew she had to go
which of you
will I
find
next?

False Economy

Once a month,
she became a beast.
So did he.
They'd go for a run,
share a meal,
then go for a swim
under the bright bright moon.
Each made sure
the other was clean;
they were back not long after dawn
to pay the baby sitter.

Got an idea, he said, later.
We could come back early,
save some money.

Idiot.
You know how hard
it was to find a good sitter?

The Young Teacher Gets Her Nails Done

She's looking fit,
With that smile men die for,
But these nails are almost claws;
It's too early for that, and off-putting
At elementary school,
And the corner store.
The handsome manicurist exclaims
Over her strong healthy nails;
She just smiles, lets him make a date
To go dancing with her Saturday night.
There's a full moon Friday,
But she might hold off til Saturday.
He's looking good enough to eat right now,
Even with human teeth.

Dating Has its Hazards

The handsome new neighbor
invited Sally for a moonlit run,
night so bright,
she could see the look in his eye,
she could see everything,
what sharp sharp teeth you have,
he said, when she smiled,
it was a shame,
he was so cute,
but she knew it couldn't last,
besides,
by now the cubs must be starving.

An Ill Wind

Cretaceous nightwalkers
look to the sun-bright South,
sink to their hideyholes;
the 10-year winter,
sulfuric acid rain,
no problem for those
who shun the sun.

Dark days following,
sucking protorats
to husks in their burrows,
drinking the last dinos
like there was no tomorrow
(for them, there wasn't);
down the years,
passing nosferatophage,
to all creatures primate.

Lovers of the moon,
blinking dirt
from newly opened eyes,
finally post-human.

The Werewolf Explanation

It comes upon him swiftly, this
Change of which I speak. You
Might think that as the moon waxes
His palms would prickle,
His nails lengthen and thicken into claws,
His jaw grow into a muzzle.
But no.
Mathematicians call it a cusp:
That point where everything changes.

Let me give you an analogy:
The salt shaker can be pushed just so far,
But when it reaches the table's edge
It plummets to the floor.
Just so, my dear, with my friend's
Affliction. When
The moon rides fat and monstrous
In the night sky, he is wracked
By a painfully swift transformation.
So powerful is its grip
That he cannot move a muscle of his own will
Until the seizure passes.
Then he is very hungry.

Why yes, my darling, the moon
Is full tonight.
I think I see its topmost edge
Peeping over the horizon.
Is it not a thing of beauty?
Why do you tremble?
We are quite alone here.
This fit will pass,
And I swear it will be swift;
You'll never feel a thing.

That's Dr. Vampire To You

The vampire didn't start out as a mad scientist,
but with humans extinct,
vampires were dropping like flies.
Chimpanzees, humans' closest relatives,
deader than the proverbial dodos,
all the other apes too,
wiped out by humans,
and monkey blood was just
… disgusting.

In her previous life,
the vampire had earned a graduate degree
in biochemistry,
so just as it might have been for humanity,
science became salvation for vampirekind.
She worked night and night,
rested fitfully by day, to rise and work again,
mixing chemicals,
rewiring arcane equipment,
splitting atoms and hairs,
manufacturing artificial blood,
(which never quite satisfied,
and killed many a test subject).

The villagers were the worst,
chasing her with stakes and torches,
burning down her lab, again and again,
ignorant and fearful
in undeath as in life,
just because a few of their fellows
had made the ultimate sacrifice,
so she could save the world.
So when she found a serum

that made vampire blood palatable,
she kept the news to herself;
a short-term solution, to be sure,
but it gave her some time,
time to find another way
to save whoever might be deserving.

And they called her mad!

The Mummy Needs Work

I mean, c'mon,
one match and we're done,
all that linen—
plus, anyone could be under those wraps:
terrorist, FBI's most wanted, you name it—
they'd never let it on a plane.

As for menacing the living,
its knees won't bend,
its hands like mittens,
mouth sealed up
for goodness' sake,
and, if it's on your tail,
matching wits with you;
maybe, if it only had a brain.

Swamped

I hate them,
their skin most of all,
dry, it is, and tender,
but I wanted a good life for my spawn.
Human female, yellow on top,
a pain in the organs of audition
for hours on end.
Let me make this clear:
I treated her well,
gave her everything but freedom.
I know they can't breathe water,
made sure she was safe while she grew,
tempted her with the choicest
tadpoles, newts, and snails;
not easy keeping her and the brood fed,
but only the best would do.

The blessed day dawned warm and misty,
our glistening jewels
slid easily from her into the birthing pool;
huh, if I'd thought her noisy before!

I let her go
when I'd received their birth certificates,
hoped she'd stay,
but the lure of civilization
tore her from us.
I raised them alone,
taught them English,
and to hide their true nature;
at last they were ready.

America's immigration policy:
our kids, USian mother or no,
no more citizens
than a Central-American refugee,
my progeny, undocumented fugitives
from anglers and propellers,
condemned to a life on the swim,
no voting,
   3-bedroom ranch,
      or manicured lawn:
this means war!

Sling Shot

It's hard to feed the family;
your boys are shooting up like weeds,
and those sheep, so fat and tasty;
you only took two.
Then, hands full,
you met this shepherd boy.

Now, the clouds look down,
you don't look up,
your face alternately shadowed
and glowing in the sun.

The little wife waits in vain,
firelight streaming out the open door,
a huge apple pie,
smelling of cinnamon, sweet,
slowly growing cold.

And you,
dent in your forehead,
no more fees or fies,
foes either,
nothing but a king-size seat
at the groaning board,
where mead pours and pours again,
platters are piled high with beef and mutton,
and your memories of sun,
two strong young boys,
wife's warm arms and lips,
gently fade away.

I'm A Stranger Here Myself

People scream and run:
Is that accepted behavior here?
I just want conversation,
A friendly game of cards,
Intercourse, the social kind,
Maybe a meal.

I dress nicely,
Speak with courtesy
on a variety of topics,
Chew with my mouth closed, etc.,
Clean up afterwards,
Always notify the next of kin.

Person of Interest

Behind the wallpaper
someone moves,
her mouth moves too,
I hear nothing,
but her teeth seem very sharp,
her breasts are sharp too;
I hope the paper doesn't tear.

She glides from room to room,
where I go, she goes,
only her face and one hand
fit behind the small strip
of bathroom paper,
but that's way too much.

When I sleep I know
she stretches the paper
above my bed, her fingertips
may tear small holes in it,
this is why I now sleep on the couch,
far from any walls,
I sleep like a baby,
a baby who dreams
someone moves closer, and closer,
under the carpet.

Flesh eating alien vampire sex on the moon

The Shummle flight is uneventful
outside the window: the final frontier
inside he sees few prospects for fun

At Dubya station he eyes vertical
lunar beauties who make earthly
anorexics seem plump

She reels him to the bar from across the room
he smokes into a wind from the planet of dry ice

The usual lines dry up his tongue
swells and his eyes water
he can't remember how to open his wallet

She pays in coins that glister in iridescent colors
she pulls him to a room and his pants deliquesce

His blind spot swells till even her
breasts vanish but he smells her
with his skin and brain

she breaks the skin with horrifying appendages
she burns him sucks him like a crawfish eats his head

They never find him
not even the bones shoot
they don't even find the room

The Mind Eater

As you are devoured,
your thoughts and memories are replaced
by a succotash of former victims,
by memories of other meals,
of boat trips you never took,
of hockey games you never saw,
of first love, last love
of betrayal, the doing and receiving of it,
of sights and sounds you've never known,
and other memories:
initial penetration of the skull,
the vicarious thrill of consuming another's
most intimate thoughts and perceptions,
of being at once violator and violated.
But soon the inexorable diminution takes over,
memory after memory, belief after purpose,
the *you* lost as the *not-you* expands,
until you are nothing at all,
save images and impressions,
remembered by someone else.

Always

in
one
of the
second floor's
empty bedrooms; no
dusty footprints, no hot breath on
his neck, yet she, always there, pressing on his chilled flesh

kept all his late wives

kept all his late wives
on a server in a locked room
visited them in VR
the little shy one
was his favorite
but he loved every one
nearly as much as Kimberly
the one currently living

Pattern of Response

The bird of terror:
two meters of beak and muscle,
King of Florida when we arrived,
them or us, baby,
just like our weird-looking cousins
with quick brains and broad shoulders,
all over Europe when the ice melted,
and the neighbors down the street,
them too.

Irreconcilable Differences

the gunshot

say why you called, she said
but I think it's pretty clear
motes of wallboard
glitter in the sun

awakened by the boom
of his emoji
the disambiguity of cheese
in fragments on the floor

reloading
spelling it out on the
front door
one hole at a time

carrier doesn't slow down
splintered post
junk mail scattered in the yard
the windows shuttered

spell it out for you

weird smells
flickering lights
pins both long and sharp
the doll begins to howl

on the grassy hill
his barrel droops
breath comes short
"you witch," he gasps

she doesn't get much
for the tumbledown house
yard sale
liquidating assets

we're getting the cabal
back together
the message read
just bring yourself

The Bad Sister

she drips slowly from the table
forms a red chalk outline
on the kitchen tile floor
I wash the knives
dry them carefully
so they don't rust
her sister
rings me
it's done
good

Smart Homes

We didn't have much, but we
bought a small lot,
ordered a house spore;
when it arrived we
planted it, watered it in good.

By the end of the week
we had a cute little bungalow
and we moved right in,
fed the house on household garbage,
grass clippings, and worn-out clothes,
tried to buy aged manure as a supplement,
but with hungry houses popping up all over,
there was none to be had.

That's when we realized,
the toilet was superfluous;
that was hard to get used to at first,
but we got a sun room out of it.
We were so in love,
life was perfect,
until I caught her on the dining room table
with some guy who'd come out
"to prune our hyphae."
Before I knew it
I had bodies to dispose of,
then two finished rooms in the attic,
and a yen for a second floor.

The Hungry Void

Remember that time,
We were nine or ten,
Playing tag in the Station,
Nina ran into the Gark ship,
And no one found her, ever,
But then you and I,
We saw her years later,
Juggling cleavers
With The Brothers Jenga,
She had four grown children
On stage with her,
Who didn't look remotely human,
Nor did she, any more,
We tried to get backstage
To speak to her,
To *what happened* and
How've you been?
But security was intense,
Someone had eaten
Minister Ahn's face right off
Just a few months before.
Then the Brothers broke up,
And we never saw her again,
Again.

Lacertilia Regina

Her raddled face; honeyed lips
rain scales with every sibilation,
stirring coigned dust devils
and reflected winks in that dark case,
carved by them as worshiped
the Lizard Queen.

Weather patterns shift, a coverlet of mold
greens & softens cities,
sinkholes suck markers into muck,
their inscriptions elide and flow
in the water-plunked caverns of the Newt,
vanish beneath draperies of crystal stone.

Papa's got a new god,
Newt glistens in the halls of veneration,
sticky blinks pass sentence
on transgressors, the monster's
four-toed manus descends
oh so heavily upon wrong-doers.

Mama doesn't make that scene,
she's moved to a higher plain;
in a cool dry windswept temple
Lacertia is reborn;
slit-pupil serenity
speaks with forked tongue,
obsidian knives drink, remember,
chants wake the moon,
sand snakes sidle; we are called.

Amoeba Girl as Teen

She used to think she should have been a guy.
Amoeba Boy would've been a terror on a date,
Many hands making light work
When it was time to put the moves on a girl.
But then again, her talent came in handy.
Locked your keys in the car?
It isn't only the Law that has long arms.
Need to spill a drink on someone across the room,
Or spy on your boyfriend?
A.G. is there to help.
Pie-eating contests?
Lay your bets, boys: she's all over that.

But that was high school.

When she got her consciousness raised in college
It was a whole different ball game.
She learned about the glass ceiling,
Force feeding of suffragettes,
The sexual imbalance on death row,
And the surprising prevalence of
Unreported domestic violence.
That's how Amoeba Girl became the Amorphous Avenger,
But that's another story.

Boa Boy Sends His Regrets

Red moon draws the lycanthrope
a hairy slavering mess
I think the silver vampire moon's
enchantment says it best

on this world of twenty moons
a melee in the sky
everybody's beast inside
comes out when its moon's high

that's why, my lovely mongoose girl
our moons both shining bright
I have to break my date with you
I'll dine alone tonight

Corn Boy

warm wind blowing
his cornsilk hair
blue eyes wide

old woman can use some help
if the tall young man will work

he grows stronger
with each row hoed
muscles swell

good farm food
fills his plate each night
sleepy by sundown

his harvest dance honey
her blonde hair and ripe body

coupling in furrows
soon their love is
blowing in the wind

The Brown-Paper Princess

Never gets to go for walks in the rain,
must be very careful with her quill pen,
isn't allowed to eat anything sticky,
or soup, only biscuits and dry toast,
really wants a chiffon dress but,
never finds anything that fits in ordinary stores,
is ostracized by the bleached-paper girls,
doesn't care, much,
makes her own clothes from a kraft-paper roll,
is her own kite, unraveled the string
from an ugly curtain,
that's how she got away.

Second Skin

There is a lizard person
inside,
trying to break out of you;
I see it in your
unblinking stare, in your
long slender
tongue, which I'm sure is forked.

Is your skin rough and pebbly
under your clothes?
I can't be sure,
but I plan to find out
tonight, if only you'll say yes
and I won't mind,
if your claws pierce my skin,
your teeth mark my face;
I see you know it's true.

A Song for You, Ophidia

a
song
I sing
it's just for
you Ophidia
you of the powerful smooth curves
muscular iridescence; you could swallow me whole
but
you
will not
not today;
your children spill out
of you, dart away from your jaws
your dinner squeaks, once, and I bow before you, always

Trip Trap

A troll can matriculate:
hunch down and smile with closed lips,
wear a broad-brimmed hat on sunny days,
change my diet to Jamaican food,
major in architecture or hydrology.

Drank too much at a frat party,
went way too far with a cute flautist,
turned out she liked short and stout
and not being able to conceive,
didn't mind I couldn't dance,
and took long long showers.

Meeting the parents was awkward
(mine: stony silence;
hers thought I was Italian),
we forged a new alliance.

I made the swim team
(I know, right!),
medaled at State;
she, marching band,
law school, prestigious gig on Main Street,
City Council, state House.

Well, eventually it all came out,
me a fabulous creature,
not even human, really,
and the whole billy-goat thing,
she had to choose: public service or love.

That didn't turn out too well,
and … "Hey, you kids, get offa my bridge!
"Don't make me come up there!"

The Successful Suitor Will...

1. Remove the head

I did, but two grew to replace it,
each bigger than its predecessor;
repeat if necessary, it said,
but now I'm up to 256,
and the Beast's castle is filling up,
plus, they're all talking;
severed heads whispering hoarsely and snarling,
new-grown buds, still attached, screaming.

Six tasks remain after this,
and I'm starting to think,
even if I manage this one,
there's no way in Hell
any princess is worth it,
even *with* half the kingdom.

Medusa's Tale

She lived alone, they say,
on an island with a small olive grove
and her collection of statuary for company.
She died alone, save for her killer,
and was ill-used after her death.
That's one version, anyway; here is another part of her story.

She walked at dawn upon the beach.
A storm had passed during the night,
the olives had lost some limbs but they would live.
On the sand much flotsam lay:
timbers from a ship, amphorae,
a tattered man, a bandage round his head.

She knelt beside him,
fingers probed his wounds, discovered he still lived.
She bore him home,
cleaned his injured parts,
wrapped linen round his damaged head,
awakened him with wine.

"My eyes," he says, hesitantly touching
the bandage that binds his head,
"are covered; were they wounded?
Who is it who succors me?"
She says swiftly "touch not the bandage—
your eyes must remain in darkness."
He is weak, lets her feed him, give him more wine,
wash his limbs, and more.
He talks, tells her of his travels.
She listens, only catches his hand if it should
stray too near the bandage on his head,
or too near her own.
Even when she beds him, she forbids him to touch her head.
There comes a day when he asks about the noise
that he's been hearing,
louder whene'er she is near,

fainter when she departs,
absent when she is absent,
a faint sussurus, perhaps the wind in sere, dead leaves.
That's when she tells him of her curse,
that he may never see her.

He laughs.
"Oh joyous day!" he cries,
"that my infirmity should bring me joy at last.
My sight was taken from me years ago,
My eyes might be two stones!"
(She winces, then.)
He tears off the bandage, gazes steadily toward where he
hears
her breath, then reaches for her cheek.
She does not stay his hand, which reads the contours
of her face, her ophidian hair,
he smiles, draws her lips to his.

Later, she allows the tears to fall.

The tale does not say they lived happily ever after;
her sightless consort was mortal after all,
and must have lived only a few decades at most.
She died alone (save for her killer), they say,
not far from her dead lover's grave, most likely,
and mayhap she thought it time.

Persephone Makes Her Move

The young Queen of the Underworld,
She hears the dead whispering,
No matter how far away,
No matter how quiet.

They know things,
So when Hades talks his way into the pants
Of another immortal ingenue,
With stars in her eyes,
Whose body slave tells her dying aunt
Every lurid detail,
Pretty soon the Queen knows
More than she wanted, really,
About what her Lord gets up to
When he's away.
She recruits a few warrior shades,
They meet H at the Styx's nether shore,
Coming home from his young lover's bed,
Stave in his boat, his head, and all with him,

Fill the boat with stones,
Sink it in the river that has no floor.

Persephone could return to light,
Her mom would probably banish winter,
But how many young women
Choose to crawl back
Under Mama's thumb?

So, Persephone's still down there,
Comforting the dead,
Ruling with a firm hand,
Taking a succession of shades to bed,
None long enough for any to think
They might step into her shoes.

Meanwhile, Hades is sinking still,
Farther and farther from what passes for light
in the Underworld,
Or maybe he has reached
That inaccessible, desolate land,
Where Gods go to die.

Beats the Alternative

The two kids stumbled on,
Our real mother wouldn't have done us like this,
the boy whined, through sniffles,
his sister wasn't sure,
but patted his head,
feeding him the last dry crust,
and dragging him down the path
when he dug in his heels.

Big trees leaned in,
oaks, hickories, scraggly pines,
stretching bent and knobby arms
from one side and the other;
roots across the path
reared up in knobs like fists.

In places, the path would fork,
the sister chose the broader branch each time,
but the path soon wriggled like a snake,
threading its way among
ever stouter and more misshapen boles.

Little Hans cried,
she carried him for a time,
but when her arms began to tremble,
and she knew she couldn't go much farther,
she came upon a clearing,
and she set him down.

A thatched hut towered over them
on two gigantic scaled legs,
no ladder, the girl said, *can't reach;*
her brother hid his face against her chest,

don't wanna, he wailed;
the hut leaned forward, crouched low,
a voice came from the dark doorway,
now easily accessible to short legs:
Get in.

Marooned

A pirate maid,
skull but no X bones,
firm flesh below:
it's the stuff of nightmares,
but wide awake I was,
and not a ship in sight.
There's been no sea here for
300 million years or more.
I showed her some fossils,
her skull nodded,
then shook side to side;
the meaning unclear
until she put her hand on me,
began to undo buttons.
If she thought it strange,
her and me together,
she gave no sign.
She turned some fossils in her hand:
I showed her sea lilies,
the ridged shells of brachiopods,
and divers creatures
signaling a milk-warm, ancient ocean.
She seemed to nod agreement
and I noticed she was with child;
she hadn't been, an hour before,
I felt her hand upon my cheek,
blinked a long, slow blink;
suddenly they upped sails,
she and her small sailor boy.

The ancient sea up to my knees; tide rising fast,
I held notebook and camera high
and sloshed toward shore—
awoke upon the fossil bed, my clothing dry,
the only trace she left
some marks on me,
and a fleeting musky scent.

Short Poems

a great eye blinks
suckered arms coil/uncoil
as he scans the menu

we burst forth
now to choose a system
for our young

we use scales and all
it's not like they have
a real language

the Altairian's fridge
I never thought to see you here
your head, anyway

diplomatic party served
frozen, grated
garnished

left my late father's
DVD on the dash
in the summer sun
hauled in for manslaughter
again

Captain dead planetside:
send a replacement from transporter data bank,
and a couple of redshirts   again

coughing starts after
the radio falls silent
Antarctica base

Emy's doll
has 2 arms, 2 legs
poor crippled thing

first-gen hybrid
screaming when she sees
his mouths

guests admiring
uncanny statuary
the Ambassador lifts its veil

a full moon rising
the dog knows
it's my night to howl

Beast never learned
how to speak to women
Beauty plaiting his silken fur

anniversary
of your death
something knocks on my door

breaking through the lid
grateful I didn't choose
cremation

the late prince
exfoliating across
the dance floor

David emerged from the soil in human-seeming garb in a previous century. He writes mainly autobiographical poetry, most of which is composed during long hours waiting for instructions from our Saggitarian overlords.

His cat regards him with suspicion, with good reason.

His poetry has been published in Asimov's, Night Cry, Star*line, Strange Horizons and many others.

Contact him at jopnquog@gmail.com

"Outside of a dog, a book is man's best friend;
inside of a dog, it's too dark to read."
— Groucho Marx

All poems not listed below are first published in this book.

"a full moon rising," Dreams and Nightmares
"a great eye blinks," Inverted Folk
A Song For You, Ophidia, Scifaikuest
A Virus Takes the Mike under review Aphelion query mid june?
A Visitor from Yuggoth, Star*line
Absolute, Star*line
Always, Dreams and Nightmares blog
Amoeba Girl As Teen, The Egg Show
"anniversary," Star*line
Bah, Bah, Black Goat, The Simian Transcript
"Beast never learned," Star*line
Boa Boy Sends His Regrets, Star*line
"breaking through the lid," Star*line
"Captain dead planetside," Star*line
Changeling, Star*line
Coming Back, Dissections
Content, Dreams and Nightmares blog
Corn Boy, The Shantytown Anomaly
Dating Has Its Hazards, Star*line
Diplomatic Incident, Kaleidotrope
"diplomatic party served," Dreams and Nightmares blog
Divine Intervention, Polu Texni
"Emy's doll," Star*line
"first-gen hybrid," Dreams and Nightmares blog
Flesh Eating Alien Vampire Sex On The Moon, hungur
"guests admiring," Dreams and Nightmares blog
Instar, Eldritch Science
Klarkash Ton and the Prophet of Doom, Poetry Life and Times
Korean Fuel Train Disaster of 2004, I Don't Know What *You're* Having
Lacertilia Regina, Songs of Eretz
"left my late father's," Star*line
Lights Over the Midnight Desert, Eye To The Telescope
Mars Colony 1 Under Attack, Cosmopoetry Internationals XXIV
Matters of Scale, Star*line

Bibliography

underfoot, the runaway spoon press, ISBN 0-926935-60-7, poetry 1991

a round white hole, dbqp press, poetry, 1993

The Conspiracy Unmasked, Dark Regions Press, poetry, 1994

hunger, Preternatural Press, poetry, 1996

Results of a preliminary investigation of the electrochemica properties of some organic matrices , Eraserhead Press, poetry, 1999

Y2K survival kit, smoldering banyan press, poetry, 1999

The Ruined City, gnarled totem press, poetry, 2003

Shoggoths, Sam's Dot publishing, poetry, 2003

The Deadbolt Casebook, Sam's Dot publishing, fiction, 2004

the egg show, speakeasy press, ISBN 0-9762962-0-9 ($40 entirely handmade including the paper), poetry, 2005 http://www speakeasypress.com/folded/foldedeggshow.html

I don't know what you're having, Sam's Dot, poetry, 2005

Separate Destinations (with Kendall Evans), D66 Press, ISBN 1-892958-02-3, poetry, 2005

Hasp Deadbolt, Private Eye, Sam's Dot, fiction, 2007

Drowning Atlantis, spechouseofpoetry.com, flash fiction, 2007

The memory of persistence, Naked Snake Press, poetry, 2007

Nursery Rhyme Noir, Sam's Dot, 978-09821068-3-9, fiction (includes all stories previously printed in The Deadbolt Casebook and Hasp Deadbolt, Private Eye, plus more), 2008

Night Ship to Never (with Kendall Evans), diminuendo press, 978-0-9821352-3-5, poetry, 2009

The Simian Transcript, Banana Oil books, flash fiction, 2010
Brushfires, Sam's Dot, poetry, 2010

The Tin Men (with Kendall Evans), Sam's Dot, poetry, 2011

The Edible Zoo, Sam's Dot, children's poetry, 2012

On the Brink of Never (ed.), Sam's Dot, ISBN 978-0-984692-04-0, poetry, 2012

Luminous Worlds, Dark Regions Press, ISBN 978-1-937128-92-0, poetry, 2013

SETI Hits Paydirt, Popcorn Press, poetry, 2014

Gods and Monsters, Popcorn Press, flash fiction, 2015, ISBN 9781519729446

Metastable Systems, diminuendo press, poetry, 2017, ISBN-13: 978-1-936021-57-4

Entanglement (with Kendall Evans), diminuendo press, poetry, 2018, ISBN 13: 978-1-936021-56-7

The Ambassador Takes One For the Team, diminuendo press, poetry, 2019, ISBN 978-1-936021-63-5

www.ingramcontent.com/pod-product-compliance
Lightning Source LLC
Chambersburg PA
CBHW060815050426
42449CB00008B/1674